DIANA

PRINCESS OF WALES

A TRIBUTE IN PHOTOGRAPHS

DIANA

PRINCESS OF WALES

A TRIBUTE IN PHOTOGRAPHS

MICHAEL O'MARA

LITTLE, BROWN AND COMPANY (CANADA) LIMITED
Boston • New York • Toronto • London

DIANA, PRINCESS OF WALES: A TRIBUTE IN PHOTOGRAPHS

Copyright © 1995 by Michael O'Mara Books Limited
Revised edition © 1997 by Michael O'Mara Books Limited

Designed and typeset by Martin Bristow

First published in Great Britain by Michael O'Mara Books Limited

Canadian Cataloging in Publication Data

Main entry under title:

Diana: her life in photographs, a tribute

Rev. ed.
ISBN 0-316-65022-6

1. Diana, Princess of Wales, 1961–1997 – Pictorial works.
2. Princesses – Great Britain – Biography – Pictorial works.
I. O'Mara, Michael
DA591.A45D5334 1997   941.085'092   C97-932112-3

Contents

Foreword

I ONCE WROTE that Diana, Princess of Wales, was the most loved person in the world. Now that she has been tragically taken from us, I realise that my words were not strong enough. Diana was a treasure; not just a national treasure, for her light was too bright to shine in one country alone, but a treasure to be shared with the world. The unprecedented level of worldwide grief for her has shown that the people's princess had no equal and can never be replaced.

It is so ironic that unscrupulous photographers were involved in the tragic accident that caused her death because the camera loved Diana and, when appropriate, she loved the camera.

In her brief life Diana was photographed by some of the world's finest practitioners of the art and examples of their best work are included in this tribute to her life. Also included are photographs of the most dramatic moments in her life and others which give testament to her tireless work for good causes.

In preparing this tribute to Diana I have been struck by the warmth that beams out from the Diana in the pictures – beautiful? Of course; glamorous? Naturally – but it is the straight-forward human warmth of her expression which leaves the lasting impression.

As the publisher and editor of many books about Diana, including Andrew Morton's *Diana: Her True Story* which was written with her full co-operation and was based on her own words, my own career has been closely associated with hers. I was more aware than most of the struggle which most of her life was. She knew she was special from an early age and she foresaw a troubled future when she accepted the marriage proposal of the Prince of Wales.

The story of her difficult journey to self-fulfilment is now familiar to all. What is so hard to accept about her death is that having found the freedom and happiness for which she fought so hard, she was struck down.

Now is the time for us to reflect on Diana's life and to remember all the wonderful things she accomplished. I sincerely hope that this tribute will provide happy memories of the bright star called Diana.

MICHAEL O'MARA, 1997

1
Childhood

LEFT: *The healthy glow of country air on her cheeks, a young Diana strides out at Park House, Sandringham – the Norfolk home where she spent most of her childhood.*

BELOW: *Diana's father, the late Earl Spencer, was a keen amateur photographer and to celebrate her first birthday charmingly captured his camera-shy daughter.*

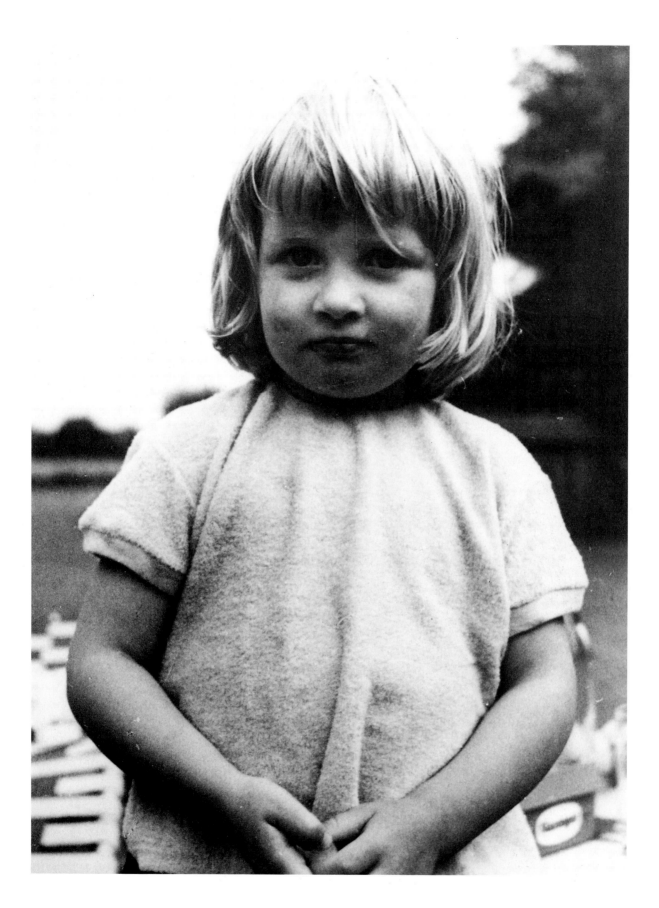

LEFT: *Surveying the scene from her pram – a picture taken from the family album at Park House, Sandringham. One of Diana's first memories was the smell of her plastic pram cover.*

ABOVE: *A glimpse of her spirited nature was captured by this endearing photograph of the cheeky toddler.*

ABOVE AND FACING PAGE ABOVE: *Diana's childhood was disrupted by the divorce of her parents, the late Earl Spencer and Frances Shand-Kydd, when she was seven years old. Nonetheless, they ensured that she enjoyed many happy family holidays with her brother Charles and two sisters, Sarah and Jane. In 1970, she stayed at Itchenor, Sussex with her mother and her second husband, Peter Shand-Kydd.*

FACING PAGE BELOW: *Diana had always enjoyed a special bond with her brother Charles, who on the death of his father in March 1992, inherited the family title Earl Spencer. He currently lives in South Africa.*

ABOVE LEFT: *Diana posed with her friend, Caroline Harbord-Hammond, by the banks of the river Seine in Paris, during a trip from West Heath school where she was a boarder.*

BELOW LEFT: *Relaxed and in high spirits, Diana and Caroline Harbord-Hammond clown for the camera in their bathroom attire.*

ABOVE: *Diana takes in the view from the top of the most famous Paris landmark, the Eiffel Tower.*

OPPOSITE ABOVE AND BELOW: *The Spencer children in a gridlock. Diana's brother Charles sits proudly at the wheel of a prized Christmas present – a blue beach buggy.*

ABOVE: *The relaxed informality of her flat-sharing days – here with Virginia Pitman – became just a nostalgic dream for the young woman destined to become the Princess of Wales.*

An athletic build enabled the streamlined Diana to win an impressive array of swimming trophies while a pupil at West Heath school. She even created a dive of her own – 'The Spencer Special'. When the family moved to AlthorpHouse, her father made a priority of installing a swimming pool for his children.

ABOVE: *Tennis was another love of Diana's – here playing on the private courts at Althorp House. A keen member of the exclusive Chelsea Harbour Club in London, Diana played often. During the annual Wimbledon tournament, she could frequently be spotted in the Royal Box and over the years was known to snatch a game with some of the more illustrious names in the game, once even playing a charity doubles match with Steffi Graf.*

ABOVE RIGHT: *The late Ruth Lady Fermoy, Diana's grandmother, was an accomplished pianist who performed in front of Queen Elizabeth, the Queen Mother at the Royal Albert Hall. Her granddaughter took lessons while at school.*

BELOW RIGHT: *Diana's step-grandmother, the romantic novelist Barbara Cartland, always gave her the latest copies of her books during visits to Althorp House.*

ABOVE: *The casually-dressed teenager learned to refine her style and dress more formally for dinner and dances when her father entertained at Althorp.*

OPPOSITE ABOVE: *Here with Alexandra Whitaker, Diana's first job was as a nanny to Major Jeremy and Philippa Whitaker. She worked at their Hampshire home for three months.*

OPPOSITE BELOW: *During a visit to her mother's home in Scotland, Diana kneels alongside Soufflé, her Shetland pony. After a childhood riding accident where she broke her arm, the Princess became a reluctant horsewoman but still encouraged her sons to ride.*

23

ABOVE: *A beauty in the making, Diana leans out of her window in a face-pack and wet towel, during a school trip.*

———————

RIGHT: *Diana striking a balletic pose in the beautiful gardens of Althorp.*

Despite the fact that she eventually grew to be too tall to dance professionally, Lady Diana Spencer practised her ballet routines in the gardens at Althorp. During the colder winter months, she could be found tap-dancing her way through the black and white marble entrance hall of the house.

OPPOSITE: *The bathing beauties. With her friend Mary-Ann Stewart-Richardson, Diana sits beside one of her favourite places, the pool at Althorp House.*

LEFT: *Relaxing days. Diana, her brother Charles and friend Mary-Ann Stewart-Richardson, engross themselves in front of the television.*

BELOW: *Her sister Sarah's legs draped over her shoulders, Diana enjoys an evening's fun with her family at Althorp.*

LEFT: *A snap of a card-game. Diana plays her hand against friend Alexandra Loyd. She was taught card games by her late grandmother, Ruth Lady Fermoy.*

BELOW: *Diana visits her brother Charles at Maidwell preparatory school, where he was a boarder.*

RIGHT: *Her right foot curled in, the embarrassment shows as a timid Diana hides behind her bobbed haircut – an early indication of the 'Shy Di' look which enchanted the world.*

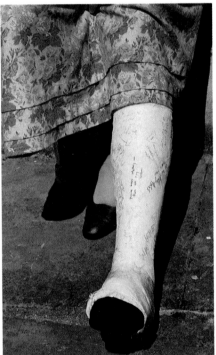

LEFT AND ABOVE: *A disastrous skiing trip left Diana's left leg encased in a plaster cast for several months. Friends and family enscribed witty and sympathetic messages to Diana over the cast.*

RIGHT: *Displaying the typical nerves and reluctant temperament of a young girl, Diana poses for a photograph at Althorp House.*

LEFT: *The Spencer girls. Diana sits back-to-back with her elder sister Jane – someone she respected enormously and often turned to for advice.*

TOP: *As a young girl, Diana's hair was light brown. However, her trademark short blonde hair became her crowning glory.*

ABOVE: *With a much-prized trophy in his arms, cricketer James Cain carries Diana from the field after winning the match. Diana and her friends enjoyed attending the friendly encounters between the local village team and Althorp House.*

ABOVE LEFT: *Viewing the world from a different angle. Diana joined a chalet party for a skiing holiday organized by her friend Simon Berry.*

BELOW LEFT: *Brotherly love from Charles. This photograph was taken by their father.*

BELOW: *Few could be immune to the attractions of Lady Diana Spencer. Certainly, Humphrey Butler, who later became an auctioneer at Christie's, looks content to have her on his knee.*

Amidst the splendour of the stately Althorp House, Diana added her own touch
of glamour with what became one of her trademarks – pearls. The maturing
Lady Diana Spencer poses for her father in a beautifully simple evening dress,
in the hallway of Althorp House before a ball in 1980.

LEFT: *In the days leading up to her wedding, Diana's hesitant glance expressed her youth and innocence, her eyes betraying the unworldliness of a girl not yet turned twenty.*

RIGHT: *Walking in Cowdray Park, Diana enjoys a chat with Sarah Ferguson, who later became her sister-in-law, the Duchess of York.*

ABOVE: *Diana at the Young England kindergarten school in Pimlico, London. This was taken in 1980 when she first captivated the nation.*

RIGHT: *Hazy sunlight streams through Diana's flimsy summer dress, famously showing her long legs to the world. But the young kindergarten teacher who had innocently posed for the photograph, was mortified.*

LEFT: *Now officially engaged, Diana started to dress the part. Photographers applauded her taste when she appeared in this stunning off-the-shoulder black ballgown, worn to a charity recital at Goldsmith's Hall in London in March 1981.*

RIGHT: *Diana cuts a dash at a polo match in Windsor Park with a distinctive sheep motif jumper and red shoes.*

2
Princess

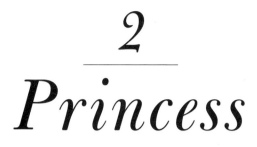

LEFT: *In a classic regal portrait, the Princess of Wales poses for photographer Lord Snowdon in 1985, effortlessly demonstrating her natural elegance and poise.*

BELOW: *Diana looked every inch the happy new mother in this official study by Tim Graham, taken only a few months after the birth of Prince William.*

ABOVE: *The early pictures of Diana show a marked difference in her facial features. In this intimate portrait, Lord Snowdon captured her healthy glow and plump cheeks – a stark contrast to later pictures where a hollow look – due to extreme weight loss – left her gaunt and pale.*

RIGHT: *Patrick Lichfield took the official portraits of Diana on her wedding day on 29 July 1981. The ceremony was broadcast to 600 million people around the world.*

LEFT: *The late Earl Spencer had only recently recovered from a brain haemorrhage when he led Diana down the aisle on her wedding day.*

ABOVE: *The joyful return to Buckingham Palace after the wedding ceremony in St Paul's Cathedral.*

RIGHT: *The famous balcony kiss that delighted the world.*

LEFT: *From the very start, the crowds came to see the Princess of Wales. Here a drenched Diana fulfils her first duties as a royal wife with a walkabout in Carmarthen, Wales. She was touched by their patience, 'The people who stood outside for hours and hours in the torrential rain. They were so welcoming . . . I was terrified.'*

ABOVE: *A sylph-like Diana bares her shoulders at an official function at the Victoria and Albert Museum, London, in 1981.*

LEFT: *In 1982, just three months before the birth of Prince William, the mother-to-be radiated happiness and good health at a function at the Barbican, London.*

RIGHT: *However, a few months after William's birth the effects of the slimmer's disease, bulimia, were all too apparent when Diana attended the premiere of E.T.*

ABOVE: *After her entry into royal life, Diana both inherited and was presented with priceless jewelry, much of it given to her by the Queen. Here, just a year after her marriage, her youthful looks were enhanced to a more sophisticated elegance with the addition of diamonds and pearls.*

RIGHT: *Mother and beloved first son. Diana proudly shows off baby Prince William to Tim Graham's camera at Kensington Palace.*

Diana's charm and natural beauty were perfectly suited to the informal atmosphere of life in Australia. In 1983 she drew admiring glances during an official tour and was pictured here in Sydney (left) and looking contemplative at Ayers Rock (right).

LEFT: *Thrilling the crowds was always Diana's forte. She had the unique talent of putting people at their ease with her good humour and attention to detail. Here she responded with charm to the electric atmosphere of well-wishers in Masterton, New Zealand.*

ABOVE: *Motherhood indisputably suited the young royal wife. Glowing with happiness, this was certainly a time of great fulfilment for her.*

LEFT: *The Australian Prime Minister, Malcolm Fraser encouraged Diana to bring baby William along on the 1983 tour, which meant that the royal couple were able to extend their tour by an extra two weeks to include New Zealand. Here Diana is pictured in Auckland.*

ABOVE: *Diana always managed to combine the purity of her youthful looks with the stunning sensuality of a sophisticated woman. She kept her make-up light and simple, allowing the richness of her jewels to add an almost ethereal look to this regal portrait.*

LEFT: *Diana celebrated her twenty-second birthday in the course of a royal tour of Canada. Well-wishers showered her with floral gifts during her visit to Edmonton.*

ABOVE: *Diana cheerfully inspects the Royal Newfoundland Constabulary during the tour of Canada in 1983.*

ABOVE: *The fashion-conscious Princess always had the knack of setting exactly the right tone with her outfits. During the tour of Canada, she highlighted her youthful beauty with simple, classical designs.*

RIGHT: *Even from the sideline, Princess Diana was simply dazzling as she demonstrated during a polo match in Cirencester.*

LEFT: *The formal elegance of red, always beautifully complemented the blonde hair and blue eyes of the Princess of Wales. Here she shimmers in sequins and lace during a visit to Norway.*

RIGHT: *A casually dressed Diana was pregnant with her second son, Harry, when this photograph was taken in 1984.*

*In 1984, Diana sported a longer, softer hairstyle. Here she
is seen visiting Dr. Barnardos in the East End of London.*

Diana in Southampton – as ever, perfectly groomed
and with a radiant smile.

A life of contrasts.
Delightful, fresh-faced informality on the ski slopes(above)
and dazzling, regal beauty for public duty (right).

ABOVE: *The perfect English Rose.*

RIGHT: *Diana was applauded for her meticulously planned wardrobe.*
On this visit to Italy in 1985 her striking outfit was the ideal choice for a visit
to the naval base at La Spezia.

*In October 1985, Diana fulfilled her role as Colonel-in-
Chief of the Royal Hampshire Regiment, based in
West Berlin. After inspecting the troops, she gamely
donned a tracksuit and hopped into a 15-ton tank
for a driving lesson.*

LEFT: *Her caring nature drew Diana into the lives of many less fortunate people. From the homeless and mentally ill, to Aids sufferers and children in need, she managed to reach out and embrace a vast range of deserving causes. Here she flashes one of her famously therapeutic smiles for the patients at St. Joseph's Hospice in London.*

ABOVE AND BELOW: *The role Diana always said she loved best – motherhood. In these two photographs taken by Tim Graham at Kensington Palace, she helps William with a jigsaw (above) and shows the two boys how to form a double act on the piano (below).*

ABOVE: *A surprise party for royal valet Ken Stronach on board the flight to Australia in 1985, brought Diana from her private quarters to join in the celebrations with her staff.*

RIGHT: *Touch down in Melbourne. Nervous laughter precedes Diana's visit to Australia.*

LEFT: *Diana was besieged with flowers when she knelt and talked to children from Macedon, Victoria. In 1983, severe bush fires devastated the area, killing more than one hundred people.*

ABOVE: *Diana could laugh at herself and didn't mind the hard-hat look.*

THIS PAGE: *A royal visit to the USA in 1985, when Diana showed a more serious mood. At Arlington Cemetery (above) and at a function in Washington (right).*

FAR RIGHT: *When Diana attended a dinner given in honour of the royal couple by the British Ambassador and his wife in Washington, she crowned her beautiful, cream evening gown with this pearl and diamond tiara, a wedding gift from the Queen.*

LEFT: *Diana smiles through a rain-spattered window at the crowds who braved the rain to see her.*

RIGHT: *Towering over her hosts, the statuesque Diana is fitted with her new kimono, a gift from the Kimono-Makers Association in Kyoto, during a visit to Japan in 1986.*

LEFT AND ABOVE: *The Princess of Wales always kept a busy diary that needed expert co-ordination and consultation. In her private sitting room at Kensington Palace, she would conduct her business meetings aided by her staff and secretaries.*

BELOW: *In the early days, designers Elizabeth and David Emanuel were favoured by Diana after creating her wedding dress in 1981. They would bring fabrics and sketches to her apartment for approval. Later, she enjoyed visiting designer showrooms herself and her taste became more diverse.*

LEFT: *At Highgrove, William and Harry were able to enjoy the beautiful countryside and keep pets of their own. Smokey the Shetland pony was an ideal choice to initiate the young princes in horsemanship.*

———

RIGHT: *Prince Harry wore a special paratrooper's outfit for this photograph by Tim Graham.*

RIGHT: *A playful pose on the doorstep at Highgrove.*

BELOW: *Diana's pride and joy – William and Harry at Highgrove.*

LEFT: *The desert Princess pictured in Oman in 1986, during a tour of the Gulf States.*

ABOVE: *'To be modern, yet keep the mystique – that is the trick', noted one observer. Diana sports a borrowed naval cap for a visit to a submarine.*

Diana's life was never plain-sailing but it presented her with exceptional challenges and excitements. Here, she was preparing to fly around the Highgrove estate by helicopter.

Diana and Sarah, Duchess of York, were skiing partners. Before they separated from their respective husbands, their friendship was especially close and Sarah's high spirits encouraged Diana to drop her formal guard on occasion. In 1987 they descended the slopes together in Klosters and clowned before the cameras.

LEFT: *Diana puts William in a spin.*

ABOVE AND RIGHT: *Diana and her sons often spent long afternoons watching Prince Charles play polo.*

LEFT: *The Princess will always be remembered for her style. She was the perfect embodiment of the spirit of the age.*

ABOVE: *Diana's cornflower-blue eyes and vulnerable gaze were unforgettable.*

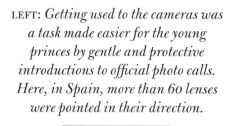

LEFT: *Getting used to the cameras was a task made easier for the young princes by gentle and protective introductions to official photo calls. Here, in Spain, more than 60 lenses were pointed in their direction.*

RIGHT: *Three years and one day old, Prince Harry meets his new headteacher, Miss Mynor, who ran the Wetherby school in Kensington.*

LEFT: *Diana travelled much of the world after acquiring her royal status. Here she contemplates the majestic sights of the Temple of the Emerald Buddha, in Bangkok, Thailand.*

RIGHT: *Diana, was a magnificent 5-feet-10-inches tall, often towering over people she met. This line-up of Australian lifeguards appeared almost diminutive by her side.*

LEFT AND ABOVE: *Diana made a great impression during her visit to Bangkok in 1988.*

LEFT: *A devoted mother and friend to children. Here, she watched Trooping the Colour with Lady Rose and Lady Davina Windsor.*

———

BELOW LEFT AND RIGHT: *The appearance of the Princess at polo matches gave rise to informal duties – presenting the prizes.*

———

RIGHT: *Diana could make an apparently random selection of casual clothes look sensational.*

LEFT: *Diana was a loyal supporter of British fashion designers. This off-the-shoulder velvet gown was created by Bruce Oldfield.*

RIGHT: *Cool in blue, the Princess of Wales and the Duchess of York cut a dash as they leave Sandringham church in Norfolk.*

The evening time was when Diana's true beauty really shone. Her tall, slim figure perfectly suited the intricate and sophisticated gowns she chose to wear and she was imaginative and bold when it came to her choice of jewelry. She often opted for fakes and was even known to alter family heirlooms.

LEFT: *Attending the Arc de Triomphe Armistice Commemoration in Paris in November 1989.*

BELOW AND RIGHT: *'Shy Di' was her label in the early days, but once the confidence came, Diana intuitively knew how to make the most of her assets. ('The Princess of Wales knows that if clothes are going to talk, less says more', noted one fashion critic.)*

LEFT: *A beautiful, casual study of Diana and her sons
in the garden at Highgrove.*

ABOVE: *Relaxing in the sun with William at a polo match
at Windsor Great Park.*

Patrick Demarchelier was one of Diana's favourite photographers.
These pictures were commissioned from him by British Vogue *in 1990.*
He brilliantly captured both the exquisite young mother (left) and the
glorious beauty of the Princess (above).

LEFT: *Observing the customs of the foreign countries she visited, Diana obeyed the Islamic dictate of covering hair, shoulders and knees in public during this tour of Kuwait in 1989.*

RIGHT: *In Dubai, her blue turban-style hat masterfully encapsulated a sense of Arabia.*

Always a keep-fit enthusiast, Diana enjoyed the national launch of 'Bike '89' on 18 April in aid of the British Lung Foundation. Making the excuse that her skirt was too tight, she politely turned down the offer of riding one of the bicycles around the park.

A thoroughly modern mum doing the school run. Diana had a penchant for American clothing – baseball caps and cowboy boots.

RIGHT AND BELOW: *The Princess of Wales with her mother, Mrs. Frances Shand-Kydd, attend the wedding of Diana's brother, Charles to former model, Victoria Lockwood at Great Brington, near Althorp on 16 September 1990.*

FACING PAGE: *In Indonesia, Diana found time for a quick game of bowls in front of an impressed gathering. She was visiting the Sitanala leprosy hospital on the outskirts of Jakarta.*

LEFT: *An unforgettable outfit. In this dazzling, beaded evening gown, Diana shimmered in her full glory at the opening ceremony for the new Hong Kong Cultural Centre on her trip to the Far East. She was the recipient of many generous gifts of jewelry and antiques over the years and here she wears a pearl and diamond bracelet, given to her by a friend.*

RIGHT: *In Lagos, she chose a beautiful, white chiffon dress, picked out with violet flowers and green leaves, for an official function.*

LEFT: *A little crumpled in the African heat, Diana may have met her match among the exotic array of tribal costumes surrounding her.*

RIGHT: *During her visit to Nigeria in 1990, the President's wife, Mrs. Babangida took Diana under her wing. During a ceremony, the delighted Princess received gifts from local women.*

ABOVE: *Diana, the instant trend-setter. When she was photographed during a family holiday on the Caribbean island of Necker wearing animal-print beachwear, it instantly became a hit with fashion-conscious women.*

RIGHT: *When her sons were young, Diana took pride in doing the school trips whenever she could. Here, she takes William and Harry to their preparatory school in Kensington for the beginning of the summer term.*

LEFT: *The film and theatre world adored Diana. On 5 June 1990, in satin and lace, she stunned onlookers for a charity gala evening at Sadler's Wells Theatre in London.*

RIGHT *'She is genuinely beautiful. I don't know why she needs me really', her make-up artist Barbara Daly once said.*

LEFT AND RIGHT: *The true professional. Whatever her pain and personal problems, Diana kept on smiling for her public.*

OVERLEAF: *Heading for the ski slopes with William and Harry. Holidays with her sons were always precious moments for Diana.*

Come rain or shine, Diana managed to make the most of every situation, even when the elements were against her.

———

LEFT: *Diana forged an affectionate and respectful friendship with opera supremo, Luciano Pavarotti.*

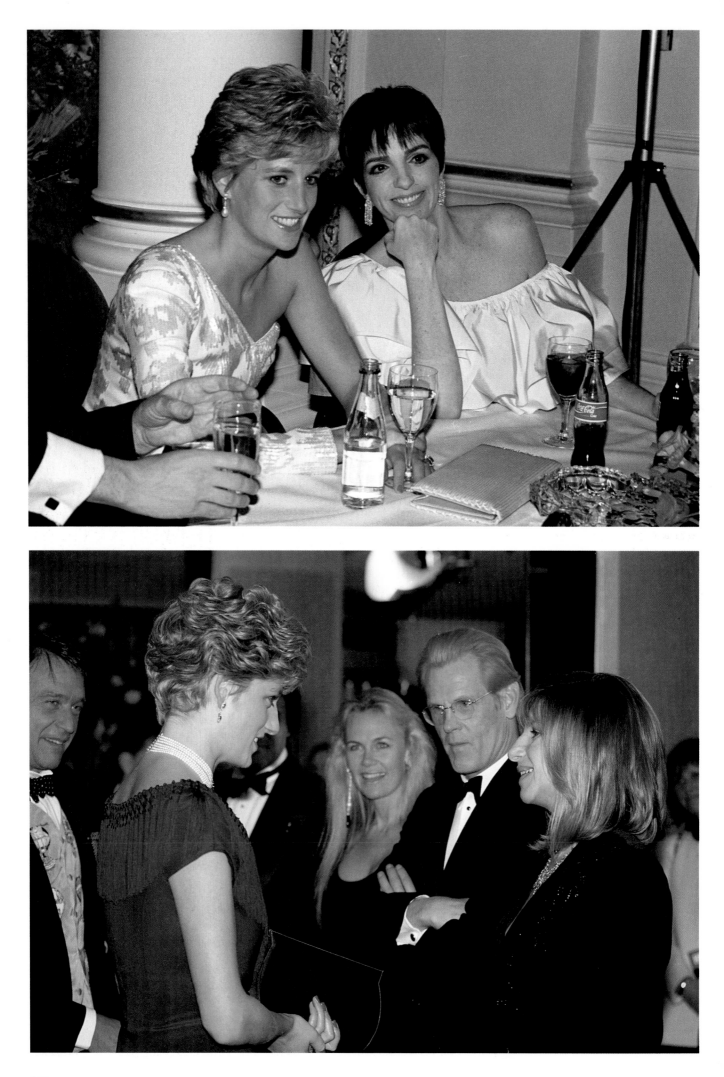

ABOVE LEFT: *The glamorous Princess. At the premiere of* Stepping Out, *Diana and film star Liza Minnelli shared an intimate chat. For a time they became close friends and shared many transatlantic telephone conversations.*

BELOW LEFT: *A starry line-up where even Hollywood's biggest names wanted to meet the world's most famous royal.*

RIGHT: *Dazzling in the dark, Diana dresses in pearls and velvet in January 1992, for the Hong Kong Gala evening at the Barbican in London.*

LEFT: *A face of serenity. The Princess of Wales is lost in her private thoughts during a trip to Cairo.*

RIGHT AND BELOW: *In 1994, Diana opened her heart in a BBC television interview and made public her feelings about her marriage and her view of her future role.*

LEFT: *Opening an education centre for mentally handicapped children, Diana gives a typically robust hug to one of the children.*

RIGHT: *Two world figures with hearts of gold formed a close alliance. Diana with Mother Teresa of Calcutta who revered the Princess for her empathy and work for the disadvantaged. Mother Teresa died only a few days after Diana's tragic death.*

3
Princess Alone

LEFT: *A battery of photographers were present when the Princess attended the Headway charity event at the Hilton Hotel in December 1993. During the event, she delivered her 'resignation speech' when she appealed for herself and her children to be given 'time and space.'*

BELOW: *On the evening in 1994 when, in a television interview, the Prince of Wales admitted his adultery, Diana attended a gala dinner at the Serpentine Gallery in London's Hyde Park.*

ABOVE: *A glittering star in the USA.*

RIGHT: *The serious and committed Diana.*
The Princess of Wales in Angola in January 1997
as part of her crusade against landmines.

THIS SPREAD: *One of the most poignant and controversial legacies of Diana's aid work concerned her dogged support for the British Red Cross anti-landmine campaign. By gently stroking the child's face in Angola (left), or through her compassion with children in Bosnia (above), Diana transcended any political conflict by showing herself to be one of the greatest humanitarians of all time.*

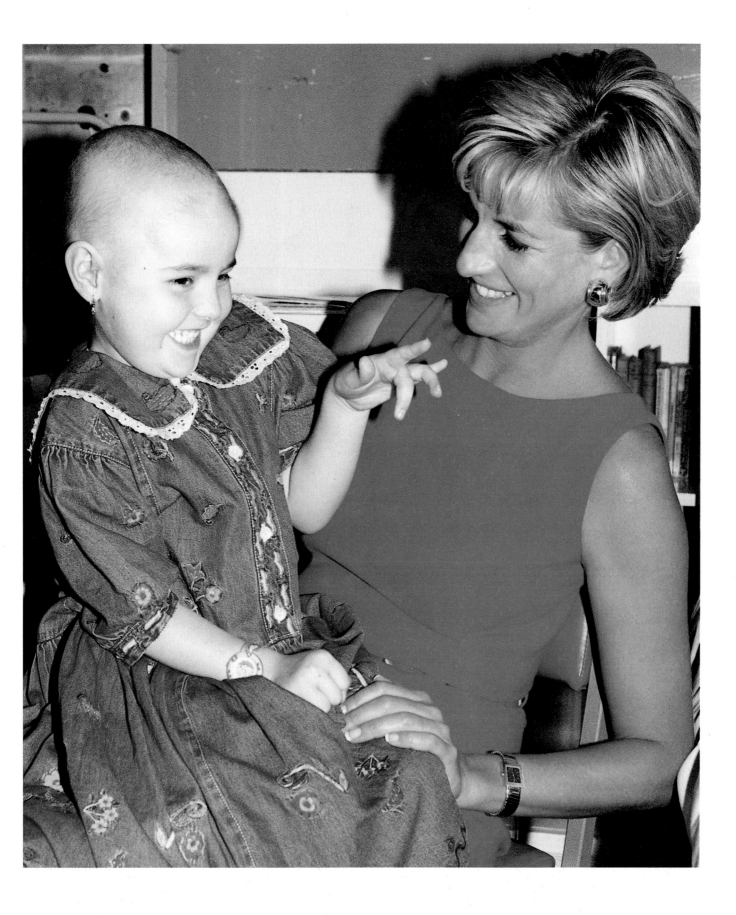

LEFT: *Diana was dazzling on the occasion of her last birthday, 1st July 1997.*

ABOVE: *In the same month, Diana visited Northwick Park hospital, near Harrow, bringing her infectious cheer to as many as possible.*

ABOVE: *A window in memory of Diana and Dodi Fayed at Harrods, the London store owned by Dodi's father.*

LEFT: *Harry and William survey the mountain of floral tributes and messages of sympathy from an adoring public at Kensington Palace.*

ABOVE RIGHT: *The bearer party of Welsh Guardsmen carry Diana's coffin into Westminster Abbey followed by Charles, Harry, Diana's brother, Earl Spencer, William and the Duke of Edinburgh.*

BELOW RIGHT: *Earl Spencer, William, Harry and Charles united in grief as Diana's coffin is taken out of the Abbey following the funeral service.*

157

LEFT: *'A unique occasion for a unique person'.*

ABOVE: *White roses from Harry, and an envelope with one heart-breaking word: 'Mummy'.*

Picture Acknowledgments

Alpha: 69, 100 (Jim Bennett); 99, 108, 158; 148, 153 (Dave Chancellor); 137 (Tim Anderson); 142 (*top*) (Dave Bennett); 147 (C. Postlethwaite)

Camera Press: 2, 120, 121 (Patrick Demarchelier); 44, 45 (Tony Drabble); 46, 48 (Snowdon); 49 (Patrick Lichfield); 50 (R. Slade); 54 (Joe Bulaitis); 126 (*bottom*) (Mike Anthony); 145 (*top and bottom*) (Mark Stewart)

Tim Graham Picture Library: 1, 40, 41, 47, 52, 53, 55, 56, 57, 58, 59, 60, 61, 62, 63, 64, 65, 66, 67, 68, 70, 71, 72, 73, 74, 75, 76, 77, 78, 79, 80, 81, 82, 83, 84, 85, 86, 87, 88, 89, 90, 91, 92, 93, 94, 95, 96, 97, 98, 101, 102, 103, 104, 105, 106, 107, 109, 110, 111, 112, 113, 114, 115, 116, 117, 119, 122, 123, 124, 125, 126 (*top*), 127, 128, 129, 130, 131, 132, 133, 134, 135, 136, 138-139, 140, 141, 142 (*bottom*), 143, 144

The Hulton Getty Picture Collection: 51 (*bottom*)

PA News: 8, 9, 10, 11, 12, 13, 23 (*bottom*); 149 (Martin Keene); 150, 151, 152, 155 (John Stillwell); 154 (Dave Cheskin); 156 (*bottom*) (Rebecca Naden); 157 (*top*) (Adam Butler)

Photographers International: 118, 146, 157 (*bottom*)

Rex Features: 42 (Steve Wood); 43 (Scarlett Dyer); 51 (*top*), 147 (Charles Sykes); 156 (*top*), 158 (Nils Jorgensen); 159

The Late Earl Spencer's Family Album: 14, 15, 16, 17, 18, 19, 20, 21, 22, 23 (*top*), 24, 25, 26, 27, 28, 29, 30, 31, 32, 33, 34, 35, 36, 37, 38, 39